HOW
TO BE
DAD

HOW
TO BE
DAD

Written and Photographed by

nick kelsh

STEWART, TABORI & CHANG

NEW YORK

AUTHOR'S DISCLAIMER A few words about saying no to your children. Here's the deal: My son is a great kid. He can be kind and thoughtful. He is also the only child of one pandering, liberal parent. Okay, two. The truth is, I have no business giving advice on how to say no. I'm not proud of this. Do not do as I say. Do not do as I do. How to say no to your kids is your problem.

Published in 2002 by
    Stewart, Tabori & Chang
    A Company of La Martinière Groupe
    115 West 18th Street
    New York, NY 10011

Export Sales to all countries except Canada, France, and French-speaking Switzerland:
    Thames and Hudson Ltd.
    181A High Holborn
    London WC1V 7QX
    England

Canadian Distribution:
    Canadian Manda Group
    One Atlantic Avenue, Suite 105
    Toronto, Ontario M6K 3E7
    Canada

Edited by Marisa Bulzone
Designed by Bill Marr, OpenBooks, LLC
Graphic Production by Kim Tyner
The text of this book was composed in Dynamo.
The author's wife is a dynamo.

Page 23: Photo by Bud Kelsh
Page 36: photograph of Mahatma Gandhi copyright © Hulton-Deutsch Collection / CORBIS; photograph of Steve Jobs courtesy Apple Computer Inc.; photograph of Abraham Lincoln copyright © CORBIS

ISBN: 1-58479-194-2

Printed and bound in China by C&C Offset
10 9 8 7 6 5 4 3 2 1
First Printing

ACKNOWLEDGMENTS

Thank you to Anne Kelsh, Chaz Kelsh, Bill Marr and Sarah Leen at Open Books, Marisa Bulzone, Kevin, Jake, and Olivia Monko, Linda Figliola, Soloman and Nailah Wheeler, Eric Kelsh, John, Susan, Sheridan, Lily, Ann, and Kathleen Medosh, Jeanie, Fenton, Sam, and Dylan Groat, Ray, Joan, and Justin Light, Caleb Bissinger, Gregory and Mia Dean, Aurelia Dean, John, Linda, Madeline, and Celia Kinneary, Martin, Julie, and Conor Loy, Oshia Russell, Toni Moore, Lynn Fox, Kim Caulfield, Jim Garvey, Joe Calhoun, Lia and Eric Reinholt, Henry Garramone, Liz Williams, Jamie Sims, Matthew, Elias, and Sophie Bartholomew, Laura Silverman, Dan, Lois, and Emily Cook, George and Linda Morgan, Dorv Schmidt, Bruce Kelsh, Doug Halverson, Noren and Sanders Ellingson, Chris Lins, Vince Johnson, Patricia Byrne, Chris Harper, Eric, Denise, Philip, Spencer, Bradford, and Caroline Jones, Court, Colleen, Emma, Claire, and Isabel Schmidt, Chantál Hardy and Charles Hardy, Sr., Woodford Cedar Run Wildlife Refuge, and to Steve Jobs for having a sense of humor.

It's okay to touch a lost baby bird. Do your best to put it in a high place where its mother—or father—will find it.

If I don't dedicate this book to my father there's going to be hell to pay.

This book is for my father.

His name is Carroll. (You got a problem with that?)

You probably received this book as a gift from a woman or a child.

Women and children have pretty serious ideas about what fathers should and shouldn't be. Those in your life may think you're a fine father. Or maybe this book is their way of suggesting you consider the quality of your parenting.

One thing is almost certain. They gave you this book because they love you. And they love you because you're the only dad they've got and the only dad they want.

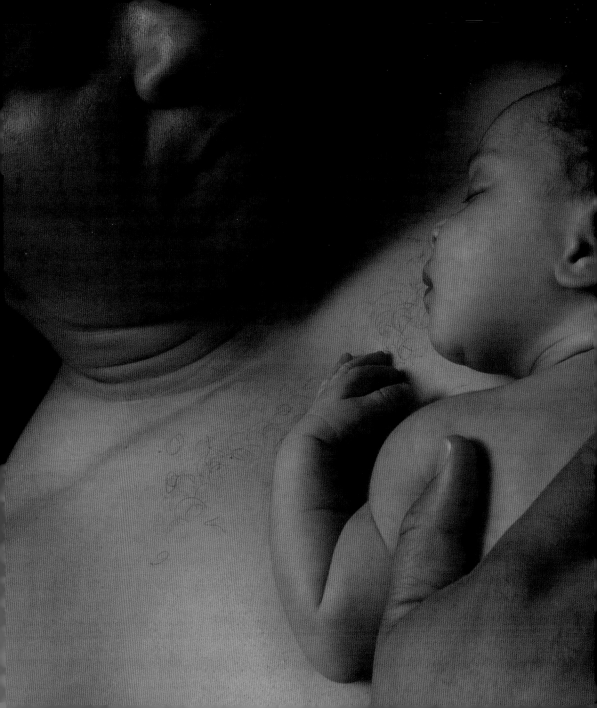

Imagine what it's like to have you for
a father.

Think of all the promises you've broken.
Think of all those times when your best
wasn't good enough. Count the lies you've
told. Now look your children in the eyes and
tell them not to lie.

Just who do you think you are to be
someone's dad?

You might be a big-time athlete. You might
be chairman of the board. You might not be
man enough to be your kid's father.

Where did we get our vision of fatherhood?
What tools did our own fathers give us to
handle the task? Where are the schools that
teach reading, writing, and fathering?

It's not always easy being a man with
children. So many of us are under-equipped.

Most of us just blundered into it. But we
knew we wanted to be good fathers,
although we weren't quite sure what that
meant. The fortunate among us have
learned that being a good father is not
something you are, but something you are
always in a state of becoming.

Men make an obvious biological contribution to parenting. However, by comparison to our female counterparts, we are physically disconnected.

There's no getting around it—she is superior in many ways. But the ability to give birth takes the cake. She birthed a baby. You never will. This can be humbling.

You can lift more weight. Your voice is louder. You do most of the driving. If someone breaks into the house in the middle of the night, you're designated point man. You didn't agree to that—it's assumed.

So what. She birthed the baby.

But here's your ace in the hole—a woman cannot give a father's love.

**The baby was crying. It was 3:00 A.M.
It was my turn.**

I'd had trouble falling asleep to begin with
and needed to be up early and reasonably
productive the next morning. I wished
that it were her turn. I did not want a
baby that night.

But after he had finally gone back to sleep
I just stood over the crib and stared.

I marveled at the source of energy that
had gripped my heart in the middle of the
night despite my body screaming for rest.

You have never faced a force bigger than
fatherhood. It's as big as God. Come to
think of it, it is God.

When I was very young, I was not allowed to leave the block. But the sidewalks in Fargo stretched long and flat and I could see my father several blocks away as he walked home from work.

It felt so good to watch my dad. I don't remember any specific thoughts—I just know that I felt good.

In the summer of 1959, my father left his two sons on the side of a South Dakota road with only their comic books. They had been fighting and screaming in the back seat and despite repeated warnings they continued to be boys.

I remember the feeling of watching the car disappear over the hill and being really, really gone.

I remember how hard I cried.

I remember my mother not being thrilled with my father.

I remember how much I loved my parents when they came back and how much I respected my father that day.

Children need to know their fathers mean business.

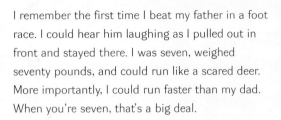

I remember the first time I beat my father in a foot race. I could hear him laughing as I pulled out in front and stayed there. I was seven, weighed seventy pounds, and could run like a scared deer. More importantly, I could run faster than my dad. When you're seven, that's a big deal.

Your children need to see you be comfortable with your fallibility.

Decades later my business partner demonstrated his superior computer knowledge to my son. "Dad," he said, "Fred is a genius." His eyes, however, said that I was not. He was on to me. My son knew that a man who was not his father knew more about computers than I did. When you're thirty-seven that's a big deal.

But things were as they should be. I could hear the echo of my father's wingtips losing ground to my Keds, and I could hear the laughter of my future grandchildren as they defeated their father for the first time.

Beating the old man is a beautiful thing. But—for what it's worth—I can still run faster than my son. I didn't say give up the ship.

My dad beat cancer in 1953. He came home from the hospital on my first birthday.

He was seventy when the cancer came back, and the early reports did not look good. We talked openly about death and the people his life had inspired. (Years later, he is alive and well.)

I told him that, after Mom, I was most concerned about my brother, Eric. He was the only one of us who shared my father's love for hunting and fishing. Even as a teenage boy he wanted to be alone with his dad and today he loves his father more than any man I know. I was scared for him and my dad knew exactly what I was talking about. He knew that his relationship with Eric was different. Not better, not more significant, just different. **You cannot spend hundreds of hours alone with a man in a boat and pretend you haven't.**

I learned a lot during that conversation with my dad. I learned that my father's feelings run deep despite the fact that he doesn't often voice them. And I learned that the only way to treat your individual children is individually. I learned that each child needs a different kind of love and it's a mistake for a father to pretend otherwise.

My father has five children, but only one Eric. And one Bruce and one Nick and one Jill and one Joel.

What does the future hold for us as fathers?

What kind of fathers will we be when we are fifty or sixty or seventy or one hundred? How can we express love to our children when they no longer sleep down the hall and they don't need us to fix their toys?

Where will we find the strength to reserve judgement?

Where will they find the strength to tolerate us?

The possibility of being a happy old father lies in giving your children the best you have today.

Encourage your children to express their beliefs on the issues of the day. Especially your daughters.

You, at the breakfast table, with the newspaper in your face: "Hey, I see the president wants to let people ride snowmobiles in Yellowstone Park. That could be bad for the environment. On the other hand, it's fun to ride snowmobiles in Yellowstone Park. What do you think?" (Encouraging her to visualize a winter ride through a park will cleverly draw her in—especially on a school day.)

When she counters with a reasonably thoughtful remark, slowly lower the newspaper, look her in the eye, and respond: "Very interesting. I hadn't considered that." You will be surprised how many times you had, in fact, not considered that.

The most valuable gift you can give your daughters is confidence. Strong women express ideas rather than aggression or submission.

I am divorced from my son's mother. She and I occasionally disagree and my son is inevitably left in what it pains me to describe as the crossfire. We do our best to keep conflict to a minimum but, like I said, we're divorced.

Here's something he does that makes me proud. He often tells me how wonderful his mother is. I wouldn't say that he defends her—she really doesn't need defending—but he does let me know that he loves her and it's clear that in his presence no one is allowed to bad-mouth the most important woman in his world.

I'm not sure where he learned this behavior, but there's something noble about it and I'm going to pretend he got it from me.

If a man can teach his son to respect women, he has given the gift of stepping outside oneself. He has taught him to care for people who, in many ways, he has nothing in common with.

Imagine the implications.

Do not take yourself too seriously.

Goof around with your kids.

It's good for them. It's good for you.

The number one factor determining whether or not an adult plays a musical instrument is whether or not his or her parents played a musical instrument. Growing up in a home where music was simply enjoyed is number two. Lessons are a distant third.

I think it's reasonable to assume that these principles apply to all forms of adult behavior.

This is not about your children learning to love the music that you love. It's about them learning to love music because you love music.

It's important that you regularly demonstrate—in your children's presence—your ability to love life . If nothing else, you're teaching them how to raise happy children.

It will never hurt a child to see a big strong man treat something vulnerable with tenderness and loving care.

GANDHI

JOBS

KELSH

LINCOLN

I asked my son to pick the perfect father from the four men you see here. He had the painfully clear option of choosing his own father over three men he has never met.

He did not. He chose Steve Jobs.

I have never met Steve Jobs. I'm sure Steve Jobs is a perfectly nice man and I bear him no grudge. In fact, Steve has always been one of my favorite names.

It strikes me as perfectly natural that I will have to wait decades for my son to recognize the perfection of my parenting. I just hope Steve Jobs lives long enough to gracefully accept my inevitable triumph.

Buying necessities after midnight is man's work.

Twenty-first century men lack dramatic ways to protect their families—fending off saber-toothed tigers among them—so we must take pride in the mundane, yet monumental, chores of daily life.

Being a father is digging a ditch in heaven. It's a lovely ditch, but it's more shovelfuls than any sane human would agree to shovel if he weren't in love.

Your children are going to go where they want to go and you cannot stop them. It's a mistake to try.

There are several ways you can deal with this painful reality. **Prayer is a logical place to start.**

Give your children all the guidance you can. But do not fool yourself into thinking they'll take it—or that they owe you for it. They were not asked if they wanted you for a father.

On the other hand, they probably would have said yes.

For a sublime period of time you're the center of the universe and you belong only to them. It's a brief sweet moment to cherish. It gives credence to the illusion that they are yours.

They're not. **They belong to the world.** You can't give your children away because they were never yours in the first place.

But don't worry. They will never belong to anyone else, either.

Have you ever asked yourself who you would die for? Really "throw-yourself-in-front-of-an-oncoming-train-so-that-others-may-live" die for?

You'd like to think that you'd be a big hero and save strangers. I think a more likely scenario is that you'd act like your shoes were glued to the pavement.
But there is a list in your brain and your children's names are at the top. You wouldn't die for them one time, you would die for them one-thousand times.

There's a bunch of people who love you for that. It's one of the reasons there's a Father's Day.

We are so much alike, you and me.

You watch too much TV. I don't express my feelings well. You think dopey little books about fathers aren't worth a damn and I don't care what you think. I want all of the same stupid stuff in the catalogs you want.

And we love our children. **So in our own klutzy, inadequate ways we are both the fathers we have always wanted to be.**

God bless us.

My father tries to look smart.
Well, time has taught me that
he doesn't actually know every-
thing. My dad's neighbor is
always talking about sports.
A conversation might go like this:

Neighbor: Did the Yanks win the
series in '54? They did, didn't
they?
My Father: "Of course. Right.
Definitely."

But I can just tell from his face
that he doesn't know what he's
talking about. Still there are
other times when it pays to
listen. Mostly he's a good guy.